# EVERYDAY MONEY MANAGEMENT

Peter Mulraney

Copyright © 2017 Peter Mulraney

All rights reserved.

No part of this book may be reproduced in any form or by any electronic or mechanical means, including information storage and retrieval systems, without written permission from the author, except for the use of brief quotations in a book review.

Disclaimer: Information provided is from the author's perspective. The author assumes no responsibility for your financial success or failure.

Cover images from OpenClipArt.org.

ISBN-13: 978-1544666204

This edition published 2018.

Everyone is entitled to this information.

You're invited to apply it.

# Contents

| | |
|---|---|
| Introduction | 1 |
| Glossary of terms | 4 |
| Principles of money management | 7 |
| Understanding your cash flow | 10 |
| Taking control of your personal cash flow | 15 |
| Do some long-term planning | 28 |
| Wealth creation | 31 |
| Planning to start a small business | 35 |
| Business cash flow analysis | 40 |
| Final word | 44 |
| A note from Peter | 45 |
| Other titles by Peter Mulraney | 46 |

# Introduction

This is a book for you if you're looking for ideas on money management because:

- you never seem to have enough money, or
- you're thinking of starting a small business.

## Money

The stuff that makes the world go around or, at least, the stuff that greases the axles of whatever mechanism it is that makes things happen in our society.

Officially, money is a medium of exchange, something created to facilitate the buying and selling of goods and services. It could be anything, and in past eras many things have been the agreed medium of exchange. Once upon a time, for example, you needed to have gold in your purse. At other times, and in other places, you needed bags of barley seeds or various types of shells. You can read the complete history of money in Wikipedia, if you're interested in the historical details, but you don't need to know any of that stuff.

Money is also regarded as a store of value or measure of wealth. That's why you see the price of things expressed in dollars, for example, and we think people with lots of money, like billionaires, are rich.

In modern societies, money is represented as a paper based currency or, increasingly, as a string of digits in electronic bank accounts connected to smart chip enabled plastic cards.

## Money Management

Whatever form it takes, money needs to be managed or, to put it bluntly, **your use of money needs to be managed**, if you are to have any control over its flow through your life.

Given the number of people and businesses that get into trouble with money, and end up using the various forms of bankruptcy available around the world, you could be forgiven for thinking that money management is a challenging and difficult task. You'd be wrong.

**Money management is a very simple task that is easy to understand.**

The problem with money is never the money. Money is not even the root of any evil let alone all evil. The problem with money management always comes down to one thing: the money manager. In your case, if you're having money problems, that's you.

## It's all about education

People often complain that we don't do enough to educate our children about money in schools. In my opinion, and I've spent more time in schools than the average citizen, they're not the right place to teach children about money. Besides, anything talked about in the classroom is always swamped by the real life examples of money management and attitudes to money children witness at home.

Think about your own money education for a moment. Where did you get your attitudes to money? What difference did anything a teacher said to you make?

So, if you missed out on money management at school and your folks didn't pass on any useful habits, what can you do? That's the question this little book is designed to answer, and you'll notice it's not a massive volume of words and techniques that you have to master. As I said earlier, money management is actually a simple task based on very few principles.

Okay, let's get started by explaining some terms you need to understand if you want to be in charge of the money.

# Glossary of terms

**Income** is money that comes under your control.

**Personal income** is the money you get paid as an employee or the money that you take from your business earnings to meet your personal expenses.

**Business income** is the money that customers hand over to a business in exchange for whatever goods and services the business supplies.

**Personal expenses** are the things that you spend the money under your control to consume or acquire in your personal life.

**Business expenses** are the things that a business spends the money under its control to consume or acquire to stay in operation.

**Business earnings** are the difference between business income and business expenses for a given period.

An **asset** is something that you use to generate income.

A **liability** is a contractual obligation to pay money to someone else. The most common form of a liability is a debt; that is, a loan that has to be repaid with interest.

**Statement of financial position** is an estimate of wealth stated in terms of money.

**Interest** is the service fee for borrowing money, usually expressed as a percentage of the amount borrowed or outstanding on the debt.

An **account** is a financial record.

**Cash flow** is a measure of the movement of the money under your control, tracked as income and expenses, for a given period of time.

A **business** is a vehicle for providing goods and services in exchange for money.

A **bank** is a business that is known as a financial intermediary, a fancy term for middleman. A bank pays interest to people who lend it money (depositors) and earns income by charging a higher rate of interest for lending that money to others (borrowers). Banks also operate the payment system that allows people to pay for goods and services electronically using plastic cards and the internet.

A **bank account** is a record with a bank that details the money you have invested or deposited.

A **credit card** is not a bank account. It's the user interface of a financial facility that allows you to borrow money, usually at a high cost expressed as an interest rate, for short periods of time.

**Personal accounts** are records of personal income and expenses.

**Business accounts** are records of business income and expenses.

**Accounts receivable** are amounts owed to a business by its customers for goods or services provided.

**Accounts payable** are amounts owed by a business to its suppliers for goods or services purchased by the business.

**Investing** is putting your money to work for you.

**Spending** is using money to buy things for your personal use or consumption.

**Saving** is putting money aside now to either invest or spend later.

# Principles of money management

## The first principle of money management: Pay yourself first

This principle is explained in the *Richest Man in Babylon*, written by George S. Clason in 1926, and in *You Were Born Rich*, written by Bob Proctor in 1984, so it's not a secret. It's not even rocket science. In fact, it's boringly obvious, when you think about it.

The problem is most people don't think about it until it's brought to their attention.

What most of us do is work all month, and then give our money to everybody else to pay for our living expenses as soon as we get paid.

It's also a general pattern of unchecked human behaviour for a person's living expenses to expand to match their income, which is why most people live from payday to payday.

The only way out of this cycle is to apply these money management principles and start paying yourself first.

The application of this principle requires that you understand that you work for yourself, even if you are an employee, and that you owe it to yourself to keep a percentage of every dollar you earn. In simple terms, you pay yourself 10% of whatever you earn, and you never spend it.

## The second principle of money management: Put money to work for you

This principle tells you what to do with the money you pay yourself. Money will not help you become wealthy unless you put it to work. $10,000 in a box under the bed is a pile of paper gathering dust – it will only increase in value if you invest it in income producing assets.

Open a separate bank account for the money you pay yourself. Call it your investment account, and have your paymaster deposit 10% of your pay directly into that account or arrange to transfer 10% of your pay into your investment account from your pay account every payday. Speak to your bank if you don't know how to set that up automatically.

These days you can get financial advice from financial planners about the best options for putting your money to work - but it's a good idea to accumulate a few thousand dollars in your investment account first.

## The third principle of money management: Live within your means

This principle requires as much self-discipline as the first, and requires a commitment to living on 70% of your income so that you can save the remaining 20% to pay for larger discretionary purchases in cash.

## The fourth principle of money management: Only borrow to purchase an asset

An **asset** is something that you use to generate income. This principle means that you only borrow money to buy something that will generate income that can be used to repay the loan.

There is one exception to this rule: buying a house or apartment to live in.

You have to live somewhere, which means you will always be paying for housing whether you rent or buy.

Ideally, if you choose to buy, you'd pay for a house with cash you have saved, but given that the amount involved is usually several times your annual income, you will probably borrow some of the money required to complete the purchase.

Because you generally don't make any income from the house you live in, until you sell it - and there is no guarantee that you'll make any money when you do, the sensible thing is to repay the loan as quickly as possible to minimise the interest cost.

# Understanding your cash flow

Before you can make informed decisions about managing money, you need to understand where your money comes from and, more importantly, where it's going.

## Cash flow analysis

Completing a personal cash flow analysis is how you get that understanding.

To conduct a personal cash flow analysis, you need access to details of your income and personal expenses. Refer to payslips, paid invoices, bank accounts, and credit card statements, to get the details.

Use a table similar to the one illustrated below to record your income and expenses for the last twelve months. This will give you a picture of the current state of play, which you'll be able to use as the basis of the next step: taking control of your cash flow. It's important to use a complete twelve month cycle to gain a comprehensive understanding of how money flows into and out of your control.

A cash flow analysis is best performed using a spreadsheet, however, if you're not comfortable with spreadsheets, it can be done using a sheet of paper, a pencil, and a calculator.

Everyday Money Management

|  | Month 1 | Month 2 | Month 3 |
|---|---|---|---|
| Income 1 |  |  |  |
| Income 2 |  |  |  |
| Total Income |  |  |  |
| Fixed Expenses | | | |
| Housing |  |  |  |
| Food |  |  |  |
| Electricity |  |  |  |
| Gas |  |  |  |
| Water |  |  |  |
| Childcare |  |  |  |
| Schooling |  |  |  |
| Travel to work |  |  |  |
| Telephone |  |  |  |
| Debt payment |  |  |  |
| Sub-total |  |  |  |
| Discretionary Expenses | | | |
| Clothing |  |  |  |
| Shoes |  |  |  |
| Fashion accessories |  |  |  |
| Entertainment |  |  |  |
| Eating out |  |  |  |
| Travel/Vacation |  |  |  |
| Car maintenance |  |  |  |
| Petrol |  |  |  |
| Booze |  |  |  |
| Cigarettes |  |  |  |
| Books |  |  |  |
| Apps |  |  |  |
| Internet |  |  |  |

| Cable | | | |
|---|---|---|---|
| Appliances | | | |
| Gifts | | | |
| House maintenance | | | |
| Donations | | | |
| Insurance | | | |
| Petty Cash | | | |
| Sub-total | | | |
| Total Expenses | | | |
| Cash Flow | | | |

Sample spreadsheet for cash flow analysis

This exercise will take some time, but if you're serious about getting control of your money, it will be worth the effort. This exercise will give you the evidence you need to take money management seriously.

For each month, record your income from all sources and all expenses. If you are an employee and your employer deducts taxes from your pay, use the net amount you receive as the income figure for this exercise. Otherwise, use your gross income and include taxes as an expense.

I suggest you use petty cash as an expense item to record the total of your spending on things like coffee and lunch.

Aim to be as accurate as possible without stressing over every last penny.

## There are two types of expenses: fixed and discretionary

Fixed expenses are things you have no choice about paying. These are for the basic necessities of life, like housing and food. Some of them will be payments you are contractually obliged to make, for example, your telephone bill. List these under the fixed expenses heading and calculate a fixed expenses subtotal.

Discretionary expenses are under your control. They are things that you can decide when and if you will spend money on them. List these under the discretionary expenses heading and calculate a discretionary expenses subtotal.

**Note:** some things which appear to be discretionary, like having cable, become fixed once you sign the agreement.

## Cash flow = Total income - Total expenses

If your cash flow for a month is positive, that is, you received more income than you spent on expenses, the answer to **Cash flow = Total income - Total expenses** will be a positive number.

If your cash flow for a month is negative, that is, you received less income than you spent on expenses, the answer to **Cash flow = Total income - Total expenses** will be a negative number.

It is not unusual to discover that your cash flow is positive in some months and negative in others.

## Annual cash flow

If your annual cash flow is negative, you are spending more than you earn.

Take a look at your credit card statements. There is a fair chance that what you owe on your credit cards will align with the size of your cash flow problem.

If your annual cash flow is zero, you are spending all of your income.

If your annual cash flow is positive, you are living within your means. If you have a positive cash flow, you should have surplus cash.

Where is it?

Is it working for you?

# Taking control of your personal cash flow

The results of your cash flow analysis are a snapshot of the movement of cash into and out of your control. How do you measure up against the four money management principles?

- How much of your income are you paying yourself?
- Do you own any income producing assets?
- What percentage of your income are you living on?
- How much debt are you carrying that is not associated with either your house or an income producing asset?

Most of us don't do too well on any measure of those four principles when we first start getting serious about taking control of our money, so don't feel discouraged if your numbers don't stack up. That's what we're here to do something about.

## Understand why you have a cash flow problem

The reason you have a cash flow problem is because you're spending all the money you earn or, if your annual cash flow is negative, more money than you earn. You probably also have credit card debt. In fact, it's not uncommon for people with a negative cash flow to be using one credit card to pay off another. This is never a good idea.

The thing to understand about credit cards is that when you use them it's not your money - it's the bank's - and you will be required to pay it back.

The thing to understand about sales that supposedly save you money is that they always involve spending your money and never putting money into your savings account.

There are two ways to improve any cash flow situation:

- spend less money, and
- earn more money.

Unless you have ways of earning extra income immediately, the most effective way to correct your cash flow problem is to reduce your spending - immediately.

I understand that there will be some things you still have to buy or pay for - all those fixed expenses. But, everything on the discretionary expenses list is something you can choose not to buy for the time being.

---

**This is where the secret ingredient of money management - self-discipline - comes in.**

## Strategy for improving your cash flow

Applying the strategy described below will, over the long term, allow you to stop worrying about money. It focuses on eliminating credit card and personal debt, restricting living expenses to 70% of income, creating a cash buffer in a savings account to fund discretionary spending, and paying yourself 10% of your income.

You can reinforce the impact of this strategy every time your income increases by sticking to your commitment to paying yourself first, restricting your living expense to 70% of your income, and saving the rest.

## Step 1: Create a budget

Budgeting is planning how you are going to spend your money before you spend it.

**Planning**

Sit down with your partner and children, if appropriate, and discuss your plan to reduce your spending to 70% of your income and why you are doing it. If your children are old enough, ask them to read this book. By involving them, you're giving them the money education you missed out on.

Start by going through your list of discretionary expenses and identifying any you can reduce or eliminate, even if only temporarily, with the objective of restricting your spending on all expenses to 70% of your income.

Review your list of fixed expenses. Can you reduce any of them? Take a close look at what you're buying to eat and at any expense that varies from month to month depending on how much of it you use, for example, electricity.

The first time you do this will be the hardest because spending behaviour tends to be habitual. You buy things without thinking too much about whether you need them or can afford them because you buy things you want. You buy the same items every time you shop in the supermarket or you always eat takeaway or take-out meals. You may be using retail therapy to cope with other life issues, and you'll probably find it difficult to cut back on your vices like smoking and drinking, and on doing things you enjoy, like going to the movies.

You might have to go through your list of expenses several times to reduce the total to 70% of your income. You may need to make some lifestyle choices, like buying and cooking fresh food instead of eating out or eating takeaway or take-out meals. You will have to put off buying some things until later, and you will have to learn to say no, both to yourself and to your children, while you sort this out.

**Note:** If food is a significant portion of your fixed expenses, put the term 'eating frugally recipes' into your search engine of choice. There are a lot of people posting information for free to help you plan meals that do not cost a fortune. It's obvious when you think about it, but one way to reduce the amount of money you spend on food is to plan what you are going to eat a week in advance, before you go shopping.

Believe me, it's better to swallow your pride for a few months than to have it taken away in court when your creditors sue for bankruptcy.

Use a spreadsheet similar to the one you used for doing the cash flow analysis exercise but, this time, plan your spending for the next twelve months so that your total expenses come in at or under 70% of your total household income.

This means that if your monthly income is:

- $2,000 restrict monthly expenses to $1,400
- $3,000 restrict monthly expenses to $2,100
- $4,000 restrict monthly expenses to $2,800
- $5,000 restrict monthly expenses to $3,500
- $6,000 restrict monthly expenses to $4,200
- $7,000 restrict monthly expenses to $4,900
- $8,000 restrict monthly expenses to $5,600

It helps if you include an amount for petty cash for each income earner as a planned expense - pocket money that does not have to be accounted for is good for relationship building.

Everyday Money Management

|  | Month 1 | Month 2 | Month 3 |
|---|---|---|---|
| Income 1 | | | |
| Income 2 | | | |
| Total Income | | | |
| Fixed Expenses | | | |
| Housing | | | |
| Food | | | |
| Electricity | | | |
| Gas | | | |
| Water | | | |
| Childcare | | | |
| Schooling | | | |
| Travel to work | | | |
| Telephone | | | |
| Debt payment | | | |
| Sub-total | | | |
| Discretionary Expenses | | | |
| Clothing | | | |
| Shoes | | | |
| Fashion accessories | | | |
| Entertainment | | | |
| Eating out | | | |
| Travel/Vacation | | | |
| Car maintenance | | | |
| Petrol | | | |
| Booze | | | |
| Cigarettes | | | |
| Books | | | |
| Apps | | | |
| Internet | | | |
| Cable | | | |

| Appliances | | | |
|---|---|---|---|
| Gifts | | | |
| House maintenance | | | |
| Donations | | | |
| Insurance | | | |
| Petty Cash | | | |
| Sub-total | | | |
| Total Expenses | | | |
| 70% income | | | |

Sample spreadsheet for budget

**Track spending**

Spending according to a budget requires tracking actual expenses so that you always know whether you are keeping to your spending plan or not.

If you are in a relationship, agree on who will be the money manager responsible for:

- paying expenses, and
- regularly tracking actual expenses against planned expenses.

A monthly meeting to discuss progress is usually a good idea. It's also a good idea to commit to supporting each other while you adjust to your new spending arrangements, and recommit each time you get off track. Keep the end goal in sight. Make it visual and stick it on the fridge, if that helps. It also helps to agree that there will be no special presents or surprise spending until you reach your target of living within your means.

## Step 2: Review use of credit cards

How many credit cards and store cards do you have?

What is the combined total of their credit limits?

Does the total credit limit figure represent more than 20% of your monthly income? If it does, and you decide to keep your credit card, reduce the credit limit to 20% of your monthly income or less.

If you need to use a card to make purchases online, consider a debit card or make sure you immediately pay off any amount you place on your credit card with cash from your savings account.

If you have either a debit card or a credit card, you do not need any store cards.

## Step 3: Pay off credit card debt

Open a separate bank account for savings, and direct 30% of your income into that account. Use the money in your savings account to pay off your credit card and store card debts until you have cleared them.

This means that if your monthly income is:

- $2,000 direct $600 into savings each month
- $3,000 direct $900 into savings each month
- $4,000 direct $1,200 into savings each month
- $5,000 direct $1,500 into savings each month
- $6,000 direct $1,800 into savings each month
- $7,000 direct $2,100 into savings each month

- $8,000 direct $2,400 into savings each month

## Step 4: Start paying yourself first

When you have paid off your credit card and store card debt, open a separate bank account for investing, and arrange for 10% of your income to go into that account every payday, that is, start paying yourself, and reduce the amount going into your savings account to 20% of your income.

This means that if your monthly income is:

- $2,000 pay yourself $200 and direct $400 into savings each month
- $3,000 pay yourself $300 and direct $600 into savings each month
- $4,000 pay yourself $400 and direct $800 into savings each month
- $5,000 pay yourself $500 and direct $1,000 into savings each month
- $6,000 pay yourself $600 and direct $1,200 into savings each month
- $7,000 pay yourself $700 and direct $1,400 into savings each month
- $8,000 pay yourself $800 and direct $1,600 into savings each month

## Step 5: Pay off personal debt

If you have other short term personal loans, use the money in your savings account to pay off those loans as quickly as possible.

## Step 6: Stick to your savings plan

When you have paid off your credit card and personal loan debt, continue to save 20% of your income in your savings account, and use it to pay for your discretionary expenses in cash, instead of using your credit card.

## Step 7: Monthly review

To avoid the trap of falling back to your old spending habits, set yourself some savings goals, and commit to reviewing your progress monthly.

## Going forward

When you have paid off your personal debts and restricted your everyday living expenses to 70% of your income, you actually have 90% of your income to fund your expenses. If you're not vigilant about sticking to your budget and savings plan, your everyday expenses will expand out to 90% of your income.

The secret to successful money management is having a plan and sticking with your plan. If you don't, you end up back where you started.

Over time, your savings plan will create a cash buffer to cover unexpected expenses and, more importantly, the money to buy things that you need when you need them.

Do the maths. It only takes five months to create a cash reserve of a month's income or five years to have a year's income in reserve, if you save 20% of your income. It takes longer, especially if you spend savings, but saving long term and spending less than what you save is how you escape from that feeling of never having enough money.

## Paying yourself first

Let's take a closer look at paying yourself first, as you may already be doing some of this. One form of investing is superannuation, also known as retirement saving or social security, depending on where you live.

You may already be contributing a percentage of your income to one of these forms of long term savings, which are designed to deliver you an income in retirement. In some countries, the law requires your employer to transfer money from your pay into a retirement savings account on your behalf, and the details of how much of your pay is going into this form of investing can be found on your payslip. Of course, if you are self-employed, you need to do this for yourself.

One aspect of this form of investing is that you usually cannot access your money until you retire. This is not necessarily a bad thing, but it means you cannot use it as a way of putting money to work for you that will increase your income in the meantime.

From my perspective, it's a good idea to invest in retirement savings and in other income producing assets. In other words, it's still a good move to pay yourself first out of the income you actually receive on payday.

## Increasing your income

Budgeting is a strategy for controlling spending and building savings, but it's not the only thing you can do. The other side of the equation is increasing your income.

Ways of increasing your income include:

- Find a higher paying job
- Take on a second job, or
- Start a small side business.

The first two options are self-explanatory, and not always as easy as they sound. Your options depend on your qualifications, the job market and what you're prepared to do.

Over the last few years, the third option, start a small side business, has become a real possibility for anyone with access to the internet.

There are lots of opportunities to explore, but stay away from anything that sounds or looks like a 'get-rich-quick' scheme, as the only person that makes any money from them is the promoter.

If you can make things, take a look at Etsy.

If you can teach a skill, take a look at Skillshare or Udemy.

If you can tell stories or write an instructional book like this one, take a look a self-publishing.

You can do some of these things offline as well. Do some research into craft markets in your local area. Make some inquiries at your local community college to see if they're looking for casual instructors. And don't overlook opportunities like multi-level marketing.

The beauty of a side business is that it can be started without a large cash investment. The investment required is time, your time, and you have a lot more of that than you think. For example, I wrote my first five books while I had a full-time day job. I found the time by giving up watching TV.

Take a look at your hobbies. Is there something that you're already doing that you could turn into a side business? Can you be of service to someone else? If you can, there's a business opportunity there.

Many side businesses start out small and generate very little income, but there's nothing to stop you from growing one into a regular income stream to supplement your existing income.

Remember, it's an option. It's up to you what you do with it.

Sometimes, the only thing holding you back are your beliefs about money. You can change those if you're willing to explore what they are. Consider listening to Bob Proctor – you can find him on You Tube – as a way of exploring your beliefs.

## Do some long-term planning

A budget is a one year plan, based on your current expenses. Unfortunately, life does not stand still, and neither do your expenses. We have plenty of gurus telling us that we need to live in the present moment but taking a break from the present to look into the future is a useful financial planning aid.

Draw a timeline for your life for the next five to sixty years, depending on your age. On that timeline, mark off the major milestones you expect to encounter. For example:

- Marriage
- Birth of child
- Child starts school
- Child graduates from school
- Child starts college
- Child graduates from college
- Marriage of child
- Purchase motor vehicle
- Update motor vehicle
- Vacation
- Purchase house or apartment
- Update house or apartment
- Retirement

Do some research on the costs associated with those milestones. For example, put 'how much does it cost to raise a child?' into your search engine of choice. The answer you get should be relevant to the country you live in, but it might also be a bit of a shock. Fortunately, you don't have to pay upfront, but you do need to plan to pay.

If you choose some of those milestones, or if you've already made choices that will attract them, start planning how you are going to pay for them now. That's what the 20% savings strategy is about.

If you're young, it's tempting to put off saving or investing for retirement. It seems so far away, but it doesn't have to be. Another way of thinking about retirement is becoming financially independent, that is, creating sources of income that will support your lifestyle that do not depend upon you working.

Finding out how much money you need to put aside to support your desired retirement lifestyle is something else you can research online. Type 'retirement calculator' into your search engine of choice and play with the numbers to get an idea of the investment target you need to set and work towards achieving.

You don't have to wait until you are in your sixties or seventies to achieve that. That's what the pay yourself first and put money to work for you principles are about. The sooner you start, the sooner you can reach financial independence.

It's never too late to start but, the later in life that you do start, the higher the percentage of your income you'll need to pay to yourself and invest.

## Wealth creation

The ultimate objective of managing money is creating personal wealth.

Being wealthy doesn't mean having a lot of money. There are millions of people that earn a lot of money every year that are not wealthy. One of the facts of life, which I learnt while working as a lending officer for a bank, is that the more money people earn the more they spend. When people came into the bank to borrow money to buy a house, the people with the big incomes borrowed larger amounts than the people with more modest incomes. That was the only difference. Neither group was wealthy.

The aim of the game is not to accumulate a large amount of money. The aim is to increase your wealth, and wealthy people own assets - things that generate income.

Money management principles one and two are about using a portion of your income to purchase assets.

Assets come in several shapes and sizes, but even people with modest incomes can increase their wealth by purchasing assets, if they apply those two money management principles.

## Four examples of assets to consider

These examples are provided as illustrations only, not as financial advice. If you are interested in purchasing assets to increase your wealth, seek advice from a certified financial advisor before taking any action.

**A Stock or share** represents a small ownership stake in a public company. The holder of a stock or share receives income, in the form of a payment known as a dividend, from the profits of the company. The ownership share is an asset, and you can purchase shares in any publicly owned company that is listed on your national or local stock exchange.

You don't need a lot of money to start buying shares. What you need is some sound advice on the type of shares to purchase. If you're interested in owning shares, do some research online and then speak to a financial advisor.

**Real estate or property** is another commonly purchased asset. Property owners lease their buildings to others and receive income in the form of rent. The building is the asset, whether it's an office tower, a warehouse, an apartment block, or a suburban house.

You need a fair amount of money to become a property owner but, if you recall money management principle number four, you'll realize it's okay to borrow money to purchase real estate because the rent you receive helps to repay the loan.

Many people start in property by buying one house or apartment to rent, and work towards establishing a portfolio of several properties over time. One thing to keep in mind with property is that there are ongoing costs associated with property ownerships - things like repairs and maintenance, insurance, rates and taxes.

If you're interested in owning property, do some research online and then speak to a financial advisor.

**A business is a vehicle for providing goods and services in exchange for money.** A business becomes an asset, once it has a customer base large enough to generate an income that exceeds its costs.

Many businesses start out as liabilities or money drains for their owners, so you often require a large amount of money to start or purchase a business, and it's not always possible to borrow that money. Like property, a business has ongoing, and sometimes ever expanding, costs, especially once you start employing other people and opening multiple sites.

A lot of us are attracted to the idea of owning a business so that we can be our own boss, and a business can deliver on that dream provided you do your research and seek appropriate advice before you start parting with your money.

Be warned, quite a few people have lost their savings playing in this space without adequate preparation, so if you're thinking about starting a business, read the next chapter, do your research, and get some professional advice.

**Intellectual property** is an asset you can create. Music, art, books, designs and inventions - anything you can copyright or get a patent for - are examples of intellectual property.

When you create intellectual property, you can license it to other people to use in return for an income stream known as a royalty payment or commission, or you can sell the rights to use the asset in a particular way. This book, for example, is an intellectual property asset, which is licensed to several online retailers. When anyone purchases the book, the online retailer pays a royalty amount into my bank account.

The beauty of intellectual property, once it has been created, is it can generate an income stream for years without any further effort from its creator.

The amount of money required to create an intellectual property asset depends on the asset. Some high-tech ideas require considerable amounts and attract investors, known as venture capitalists. Others, like a book, only require the investment needed to purchase a laptop and the software required to convert text files into e-books.

This might be one to think about if you're considering starting a side business, but remember to do your research before you release your asset into the wild.

If you have ideas that require a lot of money to turn into reality, seek legal advice before you sign over any of your rights to someone else with deep pockets.

# Planning to start a small business

Read this chapter if you're thinking about starting a small business.

## Money management is essential for small business success

To put it bluntly, if you can't manage money, starting a small business is one of the easiest ways to lose your money.

A lot of people lose their money because they fail to plan before they start. Others lose their money because they don't track their expenses, allow customers to buy on credit, or fail to separate their personal and business accounts.

You should never start a small business without consulting an accountant and developing a business plan, and you definitely shouldn't buy one without consulting an accountant to review the figures and develop a business plan. Not everyone is honest about their business performance, so you need to check things out before you part with your money to buy your dream.

It's one thing to have a great idea. Executing that idea and converting it into cash is something you can easily delude yourself about. That means you need to do some research. Is there a market for your bright idea? How much are people willing to pay for it? There is no point in investing your savings in developing a product that nobody wants.

## Working out how much the business needs to earn

One aspect of a business plan is like budgeting, with the big difference being that you don't know what your monthly income is. You have to make some assumptions, and this is where it gets tricky. You need to do that research to get some idea of what your income is likely to be. There is no point in just guessing.

What you can calculate for a business are its likely monthly expenses. Things like rent, lease payments, the cost of supplies, insurance, loan repayments, wages and taxes. Use a spreadsheet or a chart, like the example below, to calculate anticipated monthly expenses.

|  | Month 1 | Month 2 | Month 3 |
|---|---|---|---|
| Fixed Expenses | | | |
| Rent | | | |
| Materials | | | |
| Insurance | | | |
| Lease payments | | | |
| Wages | | | |
| Loan repayments | | | |
| Electricity | | | |
| Telephone | | | |
| Internet | | | |
| Sub-total | | | |
| Discretionary Expenses | | | |
| Advertising | | | |
| Petty cash | | | |
| Sub-total | | | |
| Total Expenses | | | |
| Income required | | | |

Sample spreadsheet for business planning

When you know what expenses the business will have each month, you know how much income you'll need to earn to cover costs. If you're planning to live on the earnings from the business, you need to add your monthly living expenses, including 20% for savings and 10% for paying yourself first, to know how much income the business needs to bring in each month.

Your business plan needs to address how you're going to earn that income. That's beyond the scope of this book but it's definitely something you need to discuss with your accountant, and something you will need if you plan to borrow money to establish or buy the business.

If you're buying a business, you'll have access to the trading figures of the existing business as a guide, but remember that they will never be a guarantee - too many variables and you are not the current owner.

If you're starting from scratch, where will the money come from to pay expenses while you establish a customer base? How long will you be able to stay in business before you run out of money? In other words, how much money do you need to invest in the business to give it a chance to grow and prosper? How much can you afford to lose if it doesn't go to plan?

## Running out of money

Believe it or not, running out of money is the main reason small businesses fail. Take a look at the results you get from searching 'reasons small businesses fail' in your search engine of choice to get a feel for some of the others.

There are several reasons why businesses run out of money. One is not having enough start-up capital to support the business while it's getting established. Another is poor cash flow management, and a third is failure to separate personal and business expenditure.

To be a successful money manager in business, you need to know whose money is flowing through the business at any given time.

Just because the business has money in its bank account doesn't mean the business has any money. That money only ever belongs to the business when it has a positive cash flow.

Often, those funds in the bank are money the business owes to its employees, suppliers, creditors and the taxman. As the money manager, you need to know whose money it is at all times, otherwise, you will run out of money.

## Business cash flow analysis

Read this chapter if you're operating a small business or considering the figures of a business before buying it. The material presented here will give you a basic understanding of a business cash flow analysis. However, I strongly recommend that you engage a qualified accountant to complete one for you, especially if you're buying an existing business.

### Business cash flow

To conduct a business cash flow analysis, you need access to details of the business's income and expenses. Refer to sales receipts, paid invoices and bank account statements, including credit card statements, to get the details.

Use a table similar to the one illustrated below to record income and expenses for the last twelve months. This will give you a picture of the current state of play.

In a business setting, it's usually a good idea to look at cash flow over several consecutive years. That way you can see whether the business is growing or not, or determine seasonal trends.

|  | Month 1 | Month 2 | Month 3 |
|---|---|---|---|
| Sales | | | |
| Other income | | | |
| Total Income | | | |
| Fixed Expenses | | | |
| Rent | | | |
| Materials | | | |
| Insurance | | | |
| Lease payments | | | |
| Wages | | | |
| Loan repayments | | | |
| Electricity | | | |
| Telephone | | | |
| Internet | | | |
| Taxes | | | |
| Sub-total | | | |
| Discretionary Expenses | | | |
| Advertising | | | |
| Petty cash | | | |
| Sub-total | | | |
| Total Expenses | | | |
| Cash Flow | | | |

Sample spreadsheet for business cash flow analysis.

Remember to include taxes and all of the associated costs of having employees as expenses.

Businesses also have fixed and discretionary expenses. The fixed expenses will generally be payments the business is contractually obligated to make for things like rent, lease payments for equipment, wages and associated costs of employees, and the raw materials required to operate the business. Discretionary expenses may cover things like advertising and marketing.

**Note:** This is a cash flow analysis, so only record income actually received and payments actually made. If the business has **accounts receivable** because it allows customers time to pay, those sales do not count in a cash flow analysis until the customers pay for them. Likewise, if the business has **accounts payable** because its suppliers allow it time to pay their invoices, do not record payment of those invoices until payment has been made.

## Cash flow = Total income - Total expenses

If cash flow for a month is positive, the business received more income than it spent on expenses. The answer to **Cash flow = Total income - Total expenses** will be a positive number.

If cash flow for a month is negative, the business received less income than it spent on expenses. The answer to **Cash flow = Total income - Total expenses** will be a negative number.

It is not unusual to discover that a business's cash flow is positive in some months and negative in others.

## Annual cash flow position

If the annual cash flow is negative, the business paid out more in cash than it received. Take a look at accounts receivable to see if the difference is due to a failure to collect the money owed to the business by its customers. The business may also owe money to its suppliers, its bank, or the taxman.

If the annual cash flow is zero, the business paid out all of the income it received.

If the annual cash flow is positive, the business paid out less cash than it received. Take a look at accounts payable and liabilities, to the bank and the taxman, to make sure the positive cash flow result is not masking a failure to pay invoices and taxes on time.

If a business has a genuine positive cash flow, it's operating at a profit.

Any other outcome is an indicator of trouble that needs to be addressed with the help of a qualified accountant.

## Final word

People that become wealthy understand the principles explained in this book, and exercise the self-discipline required to direct 10% or more of their income into income generating assets.

Being wealthy is not the same as having a lot of money. It's about creating or owning income generating assets.

Remember, if you spend all of your income on your lifestyle you might have a great time, but that lifestyle will cease when your income stops.

Taking control of your money is a process. It requires commitment and self-discipline but it is not a mystery. It's actually all about self-control. It's not really the money you have to manage. As I said at the start, it's the money manager that needs managing - you and your spending are what really need managing.

You now have access to the same knowledge that others have used to take control of their money and become wealthy. My hope, in sharing this information with you, is that you'll decide to use what you have read here to become a successful money manager, and plan for your future, so you won't have to worry about your income stopping.

## A note from Peter

*Everyday Money Management* is the third book in the Everyday Business Skills series, in which I share the knowledge I gained from a forty-year career in education, banking, and government.

If you found it useful, please consider writing a review or sharing the book's details on social media to help other readers find the book.

In addition to the Everyday Business Skills series, I have several other books you might enjoy reading.

You can find details about all of my books and read my blog on www.petermulraney.com, where you can join my Crime Readers Group and download a free copy of my novella: *Deadly Sands* or subscribe to my monthly newsletter 'Insights from a crime writing mystic' and download a free copy of *A Question of Perspective*.

Finally, thank you for buying the book.

Peter Mulraney

# Other titles by Peter Mulraney

**Everyday Business Skills**

Everyday Project Management

Everyday Productivity

**Living Alone series**

After She's Gone

Cooking 4 One

Sanity Savers

Living Alone (Collection)

Living Alone Journal

**Inspector West series**

After

The Holiday

Holy Death

Whistleblower

Twisted Justice

The East Park Syndicate

**Novella**

The New Girlfriend

**Stella Bruno Investigates series**

The Identity Thief

A Gun of Many Parts

Bones in the Forest

A Deadly Game of Hangman

Taken

Fallout

**Writings of the Mystic**

Sharing the Journey: Reflections of a Reluctant Mystic.

A Question of Perspective

My Life is My Responsibility: Insights for Conscious Living

I Am Affirmations: The Power of Words

Beyond the Words: Reflections on I Am Affirmations

Mystical Journey: A Handbook for Modern Mystics

**Sharing the Journey Coloring Books**

Sharing the Journey Coloring Book ~ Mandalas

Sharing the Journey Coloring Book ~ Mandalas by 3

**Sharing the Journey Coloring Journals**

Sharing the Journey Coloring Journal

Sharing the Journey Coloring Journal ~ Discovery

Sharing the Journey Coloring Journal ~ Reflection

www.ingramcontent.com/pod-product-compliance
Lightning Source LLC
Chambersburg PA
CBHW072114290426
44110CB00014B/1912